VICTORIAN CEMETERY ART

Edmund V. Gillon Jr.

with 260 photographs
by the author

Dover Publications, Inc., New York

Published in Canada by General Publishing Company, Ltd., 30 Lesmill Road, Don Mills, Toronto, Ontario.
Published in the United Kingdom by Constable and Company, Ltd., 10 Orange Street, London WC 2.

Victorian Cemetery Art is a new work, published for the first time by Dover Publications, Inc., in 1972.

International Standard Book Number: 0-486-22785-5
Library of Congress Catalog Card Number: 71-175421

Manufactured in the United States of America
Dover Publications, Inc.
180 Varick Street
New York, N.Y. 10014

INTRODUCTION TO THE DOVER EDITION

At a time when Americans have become increasingly alarmed about the kind of land-scape they are producing, it may be valuable to see what people of an earlier period did with theirs. As the bulldozer and the smokestack seem to be conspiring to produce the worst of all possible worlds, one feels more kindly toward the Victorians, who at least provided grassy slopes for their children and quiet spots for meditation and repose.

One such peaceful spot—and one little explored till now—was the Victorian cemetery, which amounted in many towns to an additional park, for public use. Where we shun our cemeteries, the Victorian family delighted in them and could think of no better place, say, for a family picnic.

For one thing, cemeteries were at that time quite new. Early-day frontier burial (usually on one's own property) had given way, in the eighteenth century, to burial on church property—the famous village churchyard. As villages became cities, crowd-ing began, and by the middle of the nineteenth century Londoners and New Yorkers were shocked to learn of such abuses as the standing of coffins in tiers or the movement

vi

of graves. With the founding of Mount Auburn Cemetery outside of Cambridge, Massachusetts, in 1831 a new concept appeared—a wooded area ("cemetery" meant "sleeping place") specifically set aside with grassy hills, solitary grottoes, "enlivened with music from feathered songsters."

In addition to being new, the cemetery was also superbly kept up. A maintenance fee was charged, and for the first time carefully landscaped grounds (as shown in the engravings accompanying this introduction)* were possible. All of this served to heighten a new attitude of the period toward death, as shown in the very epitaphs used. Eighteenth-century epitaphs had been blunt and to the point (". . . the dirty liar buried here . . ."); Victorian epitaphs, reflecting the change from gray-slate markers to softer-seeming white marble, were more cheerful, more restrained: the deceased was "asleep," "at rest," "gone away . . ."

There was, of course, a good reason for this acceptance of death that still kept it at some distance, putting the graves outside of town instead of in the heart of it. That was the death rate, which continued to be astonishingly high in this period. Science was not to make its inroads against disease until the 1880's, and the sight of a hearse at the door or the whole town closed for a funeral was as common as the moving sight of the large number of children's graves in the cemetery.

*Engravings accompanying introduction are from N. Cleaveland and Cornelia Walter, *Green-Wood and Mount Auburn*, New York, R. Martin, 1847 (from the drawings of James Smillie).

MONUMENT TO WILLᵐ A. LAWRENCE

RECEIVING TOMB, ARBOR WATER

GREENWOOD CEMETERY.

LAWN GIRT HILL.

OCEAN HILL.

If the graves had to be put outside of town, it did not mean they were forgotten, as the large number of visitors showed. Laurel Hill Cemetery in Philadelphia boasted of 30,000 tourists a year; and Greenwood Cemetery, founded in Brooklyn in 1838, drew such streams that special carriages had to be stationed to convey the visitor to an afternoon of boating or peaceful botanical study on shore.

The large amounts of space in the Victorian cemetery were to revolutionize cemetery art, and permit the use of sculpture in a way that the crowded churchyard had never allowed. Sepulchral sculpture, with its prone effigies and kneeling weepers, had flowered in the past, but only for the rich and powerful. Now, for the first time, the average man could have the sort of tomb formerly reserved for emperors.

Whether it was England's Victoria (who was known to like large monuments) or the material wealth of the Victorians that set the tone for such displays is not known. The Victorians, with their great sense of the personal, felt that individual achievement should be recognized. It did not seem right to them that a child should have the same stone as a war veteran, or that the minister and the ship captain should lie, as they do today, under nearly identical markers. The question then became: What symbolism should be used to distinguish such different types of grief?

Artists in the Renaissance had used a standard iconography such as that set forth in Cesare Ripa's *Iconologia*. A triangle at that time meant God, a phoenix resurrection, and so on; everyone knew and immediately recognized such symbols. By the nine-

x

teenth century, however, recognition of such symbolism was breaking down, and while much of it appears in the photographs in these pages (the sheaf of wheat for someone old; the broken golden bowl; the lamb for innocence and resurrection), there were other instances in which the artist-craftsman was thrown back on his own resources. Thus an open Bible (sometimes with the text of the last sermon preached) became a symbol for a minister, or a fire helmet for a fireman. One man is represented by the whiskers that earned him abuse—ship captains by models of their ships, surprisingly detailed. A stone in the shape of a church strikes us as clever, as does a gate just ajar. But sometimes the symbols are superbly personal: a favorite gardening hat for a gardener; a chair with a book on it for someone who was a great reader.

A large variety of such symbols can be found as one turns through the pages that follow. First are shown angels—or human figures caught in some lingering, meditative moment. It will be seen that the sculptors and stonecutters found many ways (including Greek and Roman poses) to represent angelic draperies and forms.

Next come children—a poignantly large group. Specific types of graves follow: those for soldiers, ministers, ship captains, firemen, and others.

After these groups come certain fixed symbols—logs, trunks of trees, baskets of flowers, lodge emblems. Animals are shown—dogs guarding their master's graves, as well as lions, eagles, doves.

Near the end of the book one finds gateways and mausoleums showing surprising

influences: Egyptian, Roman, Byzantine. Finally there is ironwork (a book subject in itself)—chairs, fences, sofas, that in their realism remind us of an Egyptian pyramid furnished for some king's journey.

None of these symbols, however, were meant to be literal. We see the literal because we have forgotten the symbolic meaning. But to their first viewers and to their creators, the symbolic meaning was immediately apparent.

One advantage of cemetery art is its permanency. Hundreds of architectural landmarks have been destroyed, but cemetery art tends to remain very much as its creators intended it. This is a great advantage for one who might wish to do some exploring of cemetery art in his area. Not all areas are equally productive, and sometimes enquiry must be made to learn of older cemeteries within visiting distance. But usually a trip to a cemetery (such as those East Coast cemeteries listed in the Index) will prove to be worth the effort.

For one thing, the very anonymity of cemetery art forces us to look at it afresh. No one can rely upon the artist's name before deciding upon the merit of the work. Secondly, we recapture an old way of viewing art—reading its symbolic language as people of an earlier period did.

The result should be an increase of interest in this neglected corner of Americana. Many books have been written about primitive art and American sculpture, yet few, for some reason, have dealt with cemetery art, though whole generations saw and knew it long before their first visit to a museum. A second look now should prove most rewarding.

Edmund V. Gillon, Jr.

New York, 1971

VICTORIAN
CEMETERY ART

1   Laurel Hill Cemetery, Philadelphia, Pa.

2 Swan Point Cemetery, Providence, R. I.

3　New Burying Ground, New Haven, Conn.

4   Woodlawn Cemetery, Bronx, N. Y.

5 Laurel Hill Cemetery, Philadelphia, Pa.

6 Swan Point Cemetery, Providence, R. I.

7 Swan Point Cemetery, Providence, R. I.

8   Springfield Cemetery, Springfield, Mass.

9 Woodlawn Cemetery, Bronx, N. Y.

7

10   Springfield Cemetery, Springfield, Mass.

11   Laurel Hill Cemetery, Philadelphia, Pa. (*side view*)

12   Laurel Hill Cemetery, Philadelphia, Pa. (*detail*)

13   Woodlawn Cemetery, Bronx, N. Y.

14   West Laurel Hill Cemetery, Philadelphia, Pa.

15   Mt. Auburn Cemetery, Cambridge, Mass.

16   Greenwood Cemetery, Brooklyn, N. Y.

17 Laurel Glen Mausoleum, Cuttingsville, Vt. Larger-than-life sculpture of John
P. Bowman (1816–1891) depicting his visit to the mausoleum of his wife and
two daughters.

18   Greenwood Cemetery, Brooklyn, N. Y.

19   Laurel Hill Cemetery, Philadelphia, Pa.

20 Forest Hills Cemetery, West Roxbury, Mass.

21 Woodlawn Cemetery, Bronx, N. Y.

16

22 Woodlawn Cemetery, Bronx, N. Y.

23   Woodlawn Cemetery, Bronx, N. Y.

24 Swan Point Cemetery, Providence, R. I.

25 Greenwood Cemetery, Brooklyn. "Our Drummer Boy" (*Clarence Mackenzie, died 1861, at age of 12.*)

26 Woodlawn Cemetery, Bronx, N. Y.

27 West Laurel Hill Cemetery, Philadelphia, Pa. A rare example of the look into a grave. A dramatic view into an empty tile-lined subterranean chamber approximately 15 feet deep.

28 Laurel Hill Cemetery, Philadelphia, Pa. Grave of William Mullen, prison
reformer, representing towers of Moyamensing Prison (now demolished).

29   New Burying Ground, New Haven, Conn. (*detail*)

HER TWIN DAUGHTERS
PRECEDED HER BUT A SINGLE YEAR,
HER INFANT SON BUT A FEW HOURS.
PARTING AND SORROW THEY SHALL KNOW NO MORE.

30   New Burying Ground, New Haven, Conn. (*front view*)

31   Mt. Auburn, Cambridge, Mass.

32   North Leominster, Mass.

E. HAYES TROWBRIDGE
MARCH 22, 1841.
NOVEMBER 30, 1901.

CATHERINE ALLEN QUINC
HIS WIFE
APRIL 22, 1846.
OCTOBER 8, 1930.

TROWBRIDGE

33   New Burying Ground, New Haven, Conn.

34   Woodlawn Cemetery, Bronx, N. Y.

35 Woodlawn Cemetery, Bronx, N. Y.

36 Greenwood Cemetery, Brooklyn, N. Y. Grave of James Gordon Bennett (1795–
1872), editor, publisher, founded *New York Herald*. (*See Fig. 39 for base of
monument.*)

37 Woodlawn Cemetery, Bronx, N. Y.

38 Greenwood Cemetery, Brooklyn, N. Y.   39 Greenwood Cemetery, Brooklyn, N. Y.

40 Cambridge, N. Y.

41   North Leominster, Mass.

42 Laurel Hill Cemetery, Philadelphia, Pa.

43   Woodlawn Cemetery, Bronx, N.Y.

44 Rural Cemetery, Poughkeepsie, N. Y.

45 Chebogue Point, Nova Scotia, Canada

46 Woodlawn Cemetery, Bronx, N. Y.

47 Ridgefield, Conn.

48 Mt. Auburn, Cambridge, Mass.

37

49   Grant's Corner, N. Y.

50   Lewisburg, W. Va.

51   Woodlawn Cemetery, Bronx, N. Y.

52   Forest Hills Cemetery, West Roxbury, Mass.

38

53   Belfast, Me.

54   Belfast, Me.

55　Forest Hills Cemetery, West Roxbury, Mass.

56 Hebron, Conn.

57 Cambridge, N. Y.

58 Mt. Auburn, Cambridge, Mass. (*side view*)

59 Mt. Auburn, Cambridge, Mass. (*front view*)

60 Greenwood Cemetery, Brooklyn, N. Y. (*side view of Fig. 63*)

61 Lowell, Mass.

62 Mt. Auburn, Cambridge, Mass.

63 Greenwood Cemetery, Brooklyn, N. Y. (*front view of Fig. 60*)

64   Greenwood Cemetery, Brooklyn, N. Y.

65 Springfield Cemetery, Springfield, Mass.

66 Greenwood Cemetery, Brooklyn, N. Y.

67 Mt. Auburn, Cambridge, Mass.

68   Laurel Hill Cemetery, Philadelphia, Pa.

69   Quabbin Reservoir, Mass.

70   Swan Point Cemetery, Providence, R. I.

71   Lowell, Mass.

72 Woodlawn Cemetery, Bronx, N. Y.

73 Lowell, Mass.

74 Cooperstown, N. Y.

75   Woodlawn Cemetery, Bronx, N. Y.

76   Woodlawn Cemetery, Bronx, N. Y.

77   Halifax, Nova Scotia, Canada

78   Greenwood Cemetery, Brooklyn, N. Y.

79 Greenwood Cemetery, Brooklyn, N. Y. (*rear view*)

80   Greenwood Cemetery, Brooklyn, N. Y. (*side view*)

81 Woodlawn Cemetery, Bronx, N. Y.

82 Woodlawn Cemetery, Bronx, N. Y.   83 Greenwood Cemetery, Brooklyn, N. Y.

84 Mt. Auburn, Cambridge, Mass.

85   Woodlawn Cemetery, Bronx, N. Y. (*side view of Fig. 88*)

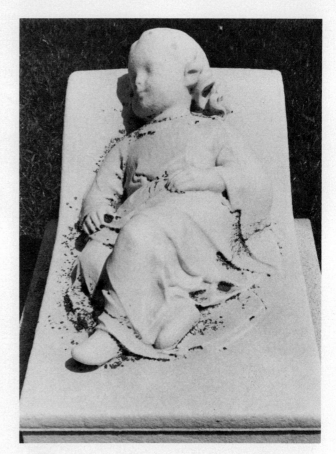

86 Swan Point Cemetery, Providence, R. I. 87 Swan Point Cemetery, Providence, R. I.

88   Woodlawn Cemetery, Bronx, N. Y. (*front view of Fig. 85*)

HENRY RUGGLES
1857

89   Greenwood Cemetery, Brooklyn, N. Y.

90 Swan Point Cemetery, Providence, R. I. (*front view*)

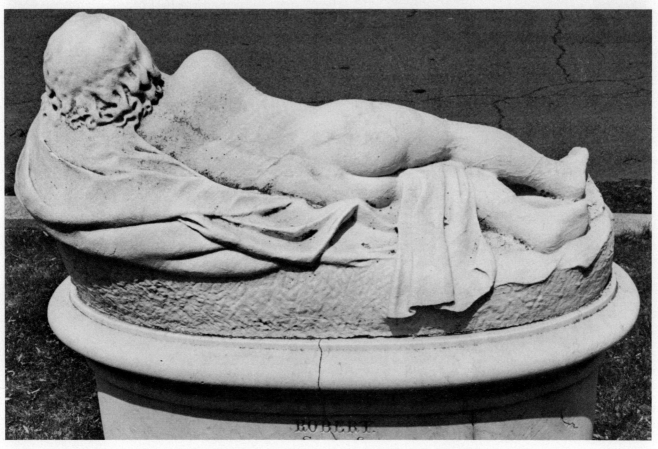

91 Swan Point Cemetery, Providence, R. I. (*rear view*)

OUR BABY

A grave with myrtle overgrown.
A lock of hair is all we own
Of what was once our baby fair.
This little golden lock of hair.
We guard that grave with jealous care.
And kiss this tiny lock of hair.
And though the tears will dim our eyes.
Our lips shall murmur "God is wise."

92   Mt. Auburn, Cambridge, Mass.

93 Lowell, Mass.

94 Mt. Auburn, Cambridge, Mass.

95 Mt. Auburn, Cambridge, Mass.

96 Mt. Auburn, Cambridge, Mass.

97   Mt. Auburn, Cambridge, Mass.

98   Woodlawn Cemetery, Bronx, N. Y.

99   Greenwood Cemetery, Brooklyn, N. Y.

100   Eastchester, N. Y.

101   Swan Point Cemetery, Providence, R. I.

102 New Burying Ground, New Haven, Conn.

103 Mt. Auburn, Cambridge, Mass. (*side view*)

104   Mt. Auburn, Cambridge, Mass. (*front view*)

105 Swan Point Cemetery, Providence, R. I.

106   Forest Hills Cemetery, West Roxbury, Mass.

107   Greenwood Cemetery, Brooklyn, N. Y.

108 New Burying Ground, New Haven, Conn.

109 Greenwood Cemetery, Brooklyn, N. Y.

110   Greenwood Cemetery, Brooklyn, N. Y.

111   Rural Cemetery, Albany, N. Y.

82

112 Swan Point Cemetery, Providence, R. I.

113 Mt. Auburn, Cambridge, Mass.

114   Greenwood Cemetery, Brooklyn, N. Y.

JOHN S. PETERS M.D.L.L.D.
WAS BORN AT HEBRON SEPT. 21, 1772,
AND DIED MARCH 30, 1858,
HE WAS ELECTED GOVERNOR OF THIS STATE
IN APRIL 1831, AND RE-ELECTED IN 1832,
IN HIS PUBLIC AND PRIVATE LIFE
HE WAS UNIVERSALLY RESPECTED.

115 Hebron, Conn.

116   Farmington, Me.

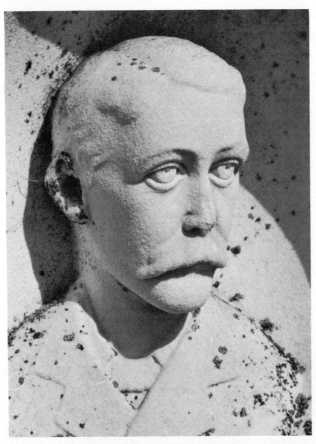

117 Oak Ridge Cemetery, Southbridge, Mass.

118 Laurel Hill Cemetery, Philadelphia, Pa.

119 Greenwood Cemetery, Brooklyn, N.Y.

120 Southeastern, Mass.

121   Laurel Hill Cemetery, Philadelphia, Pa.

122   Laurel Hill Cemetery, Philadelphia, Pa.

123 North Leominster, Mass. Grave of Joseph Palmer (*died Oct. 30, 1873, aged 84 years, 5 months*). Founder of Harvard fruitlands (*Utopian Society*) in Massachusetts. His beard singled him out for ridicule, but he lived to see his unorthodoxy become acceptable when, after the Civil War, beards became de rigueur.

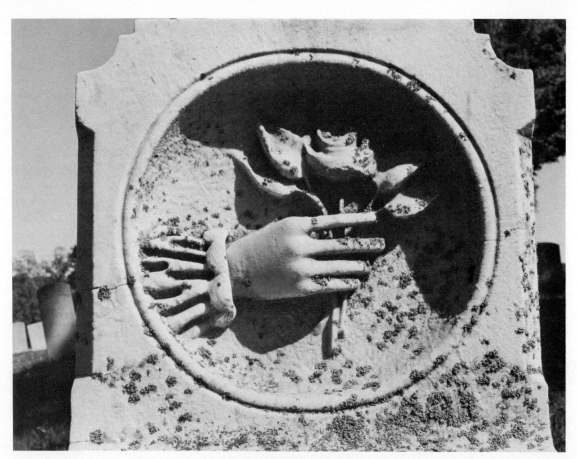

124 Willimantic, Conn.

125 North Brookfield, Mass.

92

126 Sturbridge, Mass.

127 New Burying Ground, New Haven, Conn.

128 Bucksport, Me.

129 Sturbridge, Mass.

130 Sweden, Me.

131 Rural Cemetery, Albany, N. Y.

CAPT. ROBERT J. COWDIN,
BORN MAY 21, 1839,
FELL AT COLD HARBOUR, VA.,
JUNE 3, 1864.

132   Mt. Auburn, Cambridge, Mass.

133　Forest Hills Cemetery, West Roxbury, Mass.

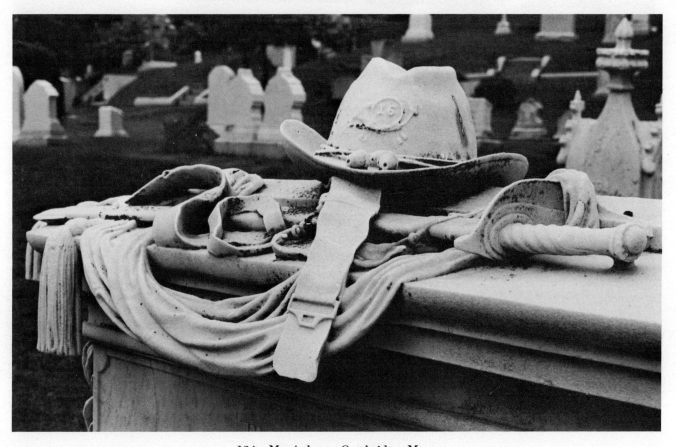

134　Mt. Auburn, Cambridge, Mass.

135   Woodlawn Cemetery, Bronx, N. Y.

HARRIET B. PLIMPTON
DIED AUG. 17, 1871.
Æ. 47 YRS. 9 MS.

136 Oak Ridge Cemetery, Southbridge, Mass.

137   Cambridge, N. Y.

138   Ware Center, Mass.

139   Cambridge, N. Y.

140   Woodlawn Cemetery, Bronx, N. Y.

141   Chaplin, Conn.

142   Mt. Auburn, Cambridge, Mass.

143   Rural Cemetery, Poughkeepsie, N. Y.

144 Rural Cemetery, Poughkeepsie, N. Y.

145 New Burying Ground, New Haven, Conn.

146 New Burying Ground, New Haven, Conn.

CAPT. HORACE G.
son of Reuben &
Betsey B. Champion.
died Oct. 28, 1853,
in Lat. 00° 34' North.
Lou. 93° 30' West.
aged 37 years.

147   Old Lyme, Conn.

148 Greenwood Cemetery, Brooklyn, N. Y.

149 Laurel Hill Cemetery, Philadelphia, Pa.

150 New Burying Ground, New Haven, Conn.

151 Halifax, Nova Scotia

152 Woodlawn Cemetery, Bronx, N. Y.

153 Greenwood Cemetery, Brooklyn, N. Y.

154   Swan Point Cemetery, Providence, R. I.

155   New Burying Ground, New Haven, Conn.

156 New Burying Ground, New Haven, Conn.

157 Quabbin Reservoir, Mass.

158 Mt. Auburn, Cambridge, Mass.

159 Mt. Auburn, Cambridge, Mass.

160 Greenwood Cemetery, Brooklyn, N. Y.

161 Woodlawn Cemetery, Bronx, N. Y.

162 Post Mills, Vt.

163 Cambridge, N. Y.

164 Woodlawn Cemetery, Bronx, N. Y.

165 Bucksport, Me.

166 Lowell, Mass.

167 Cambridge, N. Y.

168 Cambridge, N. Y.

169   Woodlawn Cemetery, Bronx, N. Y.

ANNA L. ARMSBY,
DIED NOV. 184?
AGED 24 YRS.

MARGARET E. ARMSBY,
DIED JULY 1845,
AGED 5 MONTHS.

170 Rural Cemetery, Albany, N. Y.

171 Lowell, Mass.

172 Mt. Auburn, Cambridge, Mass.

173   Swan Point Cemetery, Providence, R. I.

174   Mt. Auburn, Cambridge, Mass.

175 Rural Cemetery, Poughkeepsie, N. Y.

176 Mt. Auburn, Cambridge, Mass.

177 Mt. Auburn, Cambridge, Mass.

178 Swan Point Cemetery, Providence, R. I.

HELEN BACON
WIFE OF
ROBERT E. CONE
BORN DEC. 13, 1849.
DIED JAN. 4, 1875.

179   Laurel Hill Cemetery, Philadelphia, Pa.

180   Mt. Auburn, Cambridge, Mass.

181   North Leominster, Mass.

182   Wilton, Conn.

183   Wilton, Conn.

184   Swan Point Cemetery, Providence, R. I. (*side view of vase*)

185   Swan Point Cemetery, Providence, R. I.

186   Woodlawn Cemetery, Bronx, N. Y.

187   Swan Point Cemetery, Providence, R. I.

188   Swan Point Cemetery, Providence, R. I.   (*other side of vase on facing page*)

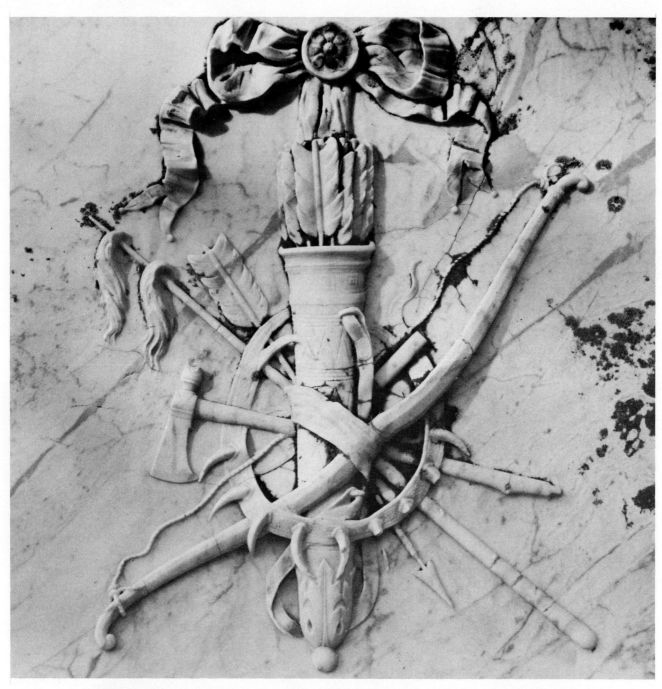

189 Cooperstown, N. Y. Grave of James Fenimore Cooper, with *Deerslayer* symbol.

190   Cooperstown, N. Y.   Grave of James Fenimore Cooper.

191   Rural Cemetery, Poughkeepsie, N. Y.

128

192 Laurel Hill Cemetery, Philadelphia, Pa.

193 Mt. Auburn, Cambridge, Mass. (*Erected by abolitionists to honor freed slaves.*)

194 Woodlawn Cemetery, Bronx, N. Y.

195 Swan Point Cemetery, Providence, R. I.

196   Rural Cemetery, Albany, N. Y.

197   Lowell, Mass.

198   Manchester, Vt.

199   Lowell, Mass.

200   Mt. Auburn, Cambridge, Mass. (*front view*)

201   Mt. Auburn, Cambridge, Mass. (*side view*)

202   New Burying Ground, New Haven, Conn.

203   Greenwood Cemetery, Brooklyn, N. Y.

204　Mt. Auburn, Cambridge, Mass.

205　Mt. Auburn, Cambridge, Mass.

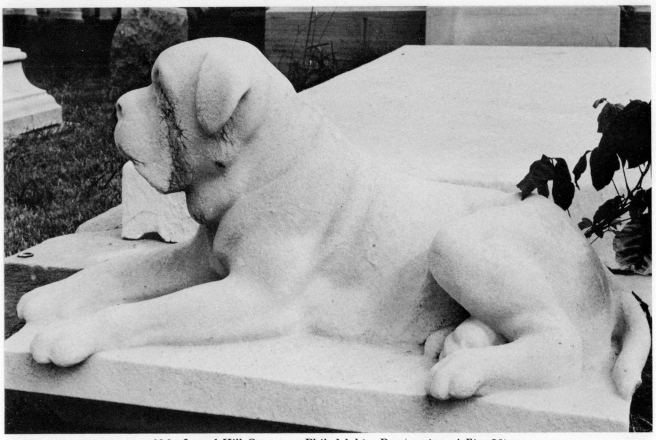

206   Laurel Hill Cemetery, Philadelphia, Pa. (*section of Fig. 28*)

207   Oak Ridge Cemetery, Southbridge, Mass.

137

208 Mt. Auburn, Cambridge, Mass. From the grave of William Frederick Harnden, founder of the express business in America. *Died Jan. 14, 1845, aged 31 years.*

209 Greenwood Cemetery, Brooklyn, N. Y.

210 Rural Cemetery, Albany, N. Y.

211   Lowell, Mass.

212   Chaplin, Conn.

213 Forest Hills Cemetery, West Roxbury, Mass.

214 Norwalk, Conn.

215 Mt. Auburn, Cambridge, Mass.

216 Lowell, Mass.

217   Laurel Hill Cemetery, Philadelphia, Pa.

218   Laurel Hill Cemetery, Philadelphia, Pa.

219 Lowell, Mass.

220   Rural Cemetery, Albany, N. Y.

221   North Richmond, N. H.

146

222   Florence, Vt.

223 Mt. Auburn, Cambridge, Mass.

224 Mt. Auburn, Cambridge, Mass.

225 New Burying Ground, New Haven, Conn.

226 Yarmouth, Nova Scotia, Canada

227 New Burying Ground, New Haven, Conn.

228 Greenwood Cemetery, Brooklyn, N. Y. Greenwood Cemetery offices, gates and clock tower. Designed by Richard Mitchell Upjohn (*son of the leading architect of the Gothic tradition in New York City*). He also designed the Connecticut State Capitol at Hartford.

229   Woodlawn Cemetery, Bronx, N. Y.

230   Greenwood Cemetery, Brooklyn, N. Y.

231 Laurel Hill Cemetery, Philadelphia, Pa.

232 Grove Street Cemetery, New Haven, Conn. Grovestreet Cemetery Gates 1845–
1848, Henry Austin, architect.

233 Greenwood Cemetery, Brooklyn, N. Y. Waiting room (*and bell tower*) for mourners in inclement weather.

234 Laurel Hill Cemetery, Philadelphia, Pa.

235 Mt. Auburn, Cambridge, Mass. Chapel and Hall of Fame, 1848.

236   Springfield Cemetery, Springfield, Mass.

237 Greenwood Cemetery, Brooklyn, N. Y. Niblo Mausoleum, for founder of Niblo's Garden, famous nineteenth-century restaurant and place of entertainment.

238   Woodlawn Cemetery, Bronx, N. Y.

239   Mausoleum at Woodlawn Cemetery, Bronx, N. Y., William Morris Hunt, architect. Replica of Leonardo da Vinci's tomb at Amboise Chateau, France.

240   Upper Clements, Nova Scotia, Canada

241 West Brookfield, Mass.

242 Sturbridge, Mass.

243 Hillsboro, N. H.

244   New Burying Ground, New Haven, Conn.

245   Halifax, Nova Scotia, Canada

246   Rural Cemetery, Poughkeepsie, N. Y.

247 Woodlawn Cemetery, Bronx, N. Y.

248 Norwalk, Conn.

249   Rural Cemetery, Poughkeepsie, N. Y.

250   Haddam, Conn.

251 Woodlawn Cemetery, Bronx, N. Y.

252   Rural Cemetery, Poughkeepsie, N. Y.

253   West Laurel Hill Cemetery, Philadelphia, Pa.

254   West Laurel Hill Cemetery, Philadelphia, Pa.

255 Lowell, Mass.

256   Rural Cemetery, Albany, N. Y.

257   Rural Cemetery, Albany, N. Y.

258 Cooperstown, N. Y.

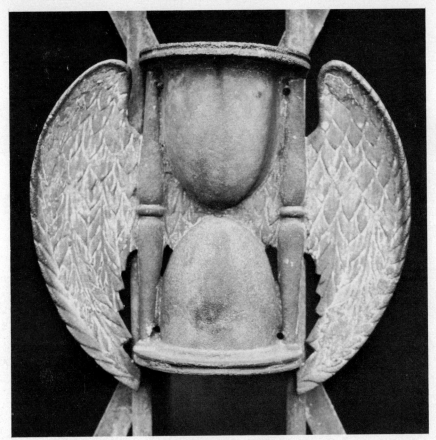

259   Greenwood Cemetery, Brooklyn, N. Y.

260   Swan Point Cemetery, Providence, R. I.

Photograph by Victor Prévost of P. Gori's marble-working establishment at Broadway and 20th Street, New York City. Courtesy of The New-York Historical Society.

INDEX TO CEMETERIES

(Numbers refer to the figure, not the page).